Quotes
for
a Dear
Friend

"The words the happy say
Are paltry melody
But those the silent feel
Are beautiful."
Emily Dickinson

"An agreeable companion on a journey is as good as a carriage."
Publilius Syrus

"I like the dreams of the future better than the
history of the past."
Thomas Jefferson

"Love is an act of endless forgiveness, a tender look which becomes a habit."

Peter Ustinov

"Treasure the love you receive above all. It will survive long after your gold and good health have vanished."

Og Mandino

"One word
Frees us of all the weight and pain of life:
That word is love."

Sophocles

"Through loyalty to the past, our mind refuses to realise that tomorrow's joy is possible only if today's makes way for it; that each wave owes the beauty of its line only to the withdrawal of the preceding one."

André Gide

"God gave us memories that we might have roses in December."

James M Barrie

"A man's real possession is his memory. In nothing else is he rich, in nothing else is he poor."

Alexander Smith

"I am only one; but still I am one. I cannot do everything, but still I can do something; I will not refuse to do something I can do."

Hellen Keller

"To be able to enjoy one's past life is to live twice."

Martial

"When the One Great Scorer comes to write against your name, He marks, not that you won or lost, but how you played the game."

Grantland Rice

"Love, all alike, no season knows, nor clime,
Nor hours, age, months, which are the rags of time."
John Donne

"When there is room in the heart there is room in the house."
Danish Proverb

"Sweet is the breath of vernal shower,
The bee's collected treasures sweet,
Sweet music's melting fall, but sweeter yet
The still small voice of gratitude."
Thomas Gray

"What value has compassion that does not take its object
in its arms?"
Saint-Exupéry

"I will speak ill of no man, and speak all the good I know
of everybody."
Ben Franklin

"All the beautiful sentiments in the world weigh less
than a single lovely action."
James Russell Lowell

"Tomorrow I will live, the fool does say:
Today itself's too late; the wise lived yesterday."

Martial

"To be capable of steady friendship or lasting love, are the
two greatest proofs, not only of goodness of heart, but of
strength of mind."

William Hazlitt

"A grateful mind, by owing owes not, but still pays, at once
Indebted and discharged."

Milton: Paradise Lost

"How much pain have cost us the evils which
have never happened."

Thomas Jefferson

"Nothing great was ever achieved without enthusiasm.
The way of life is wonderful; it is by abandonment."

Ralph Waldo Emerson

"Where you go, I will go, and where you stay, I will stay.
Your people shall be my people, and your God my God.
Where you die, I will die, and there I will be buried."

Ruth 1:16–17

"Nothing is so strong as gentleness, and nothing is so gentle as real strength."

Ralph W Sockman

"What is the odds so long as the fire of soul is kindled at the taper of conviviality, and the wing of friendship never moults a feather?"

Charles Dickens: The Old Curiosity Shop

"Man loves company even if only that of a small burning candle."

Georg Christoph Lichtenberg

"There is no hope of joy except in human relations."
Saint-Exupéry

"Forgiveness is the answer to the child's dream of a miracle by which what is broken is made whole again, what is soiled is again made clean."
Dag Hammarskjold

"Friendship multiplies the good of life and divides the evil. 'Tis the sole remedy against misfortune, the very ventilation of the soul."
Baltasar Gracian

"Bliss in possession will not last;
Remembered joys are never past."

James Montgomery

"I keep my friends as misers do their treasure, because, of
all the things granted us by wisdom, none is greater or
better than friendship."

Pietro Aretino

"We have no more right to consume happiness without
producing it than to consume wealth without producing it."

George Bernard Shaw: Candida

"Happiness makes up in height for what it lacks in length."
Robert Frost

"Silence is the perfectest herald of joy. I were but little
happy if I could say how much."
Shakespeare: Much Ado About Nothing

"He who binds to himself a joy
Does the winged life destroy;
But he who kisses the joy as it flies
Lives in eternity's sunrise."
William Blake: Eternity

"One doesn't discover new lands without consenting to lose sight of the shore for a very long time."

André Gide: The Counterfeiters

"It is not the years in your life but the life in your years that counts!"

Adlai Stevenson: Coronet

"There's nothing worth the wear of winning,
But laughter and the love of friends."

Hilaire Belloc

"One who knows how to show and to accept kindness will be a friend better than any possession."

Sophocles

"That best portion of a good man's life,
His little, nameless, unremembered acts
Of kindness and of love."

William Wordsworth

"Generosity is the flower of justice."

Nathaniel Hawthorne

"A friend may well be reckoned the masterpiece of nature."
Ralph Waldo Emerson

"Memory is the diary that we all carry about with us."
Oscar Wilde

"Kind hearts are more than coronets,
And simple faith than Norman Blood."
Lord Tennyson

"As poetry is the harmony of words, so music is that of notes."
John Dryden

"The most wasted day is that in which we have not laughed."
Chamfort

"All love is sweet,
Given or returned. Common as light is love,
And its familiar voice wearies not ever."
Shelley: Prometheus Unbound

"Your friend is the man who knows all about you and
still likes you."
Elbert Hubbard

"Man is that he might have joy."

Joseph Smith

"Memory is not so brilliant as hope, but it is more beautiful, and a thousand times as true."

George Dennison Prentice

"The proper office of a friend is to side with you when you are in the wrong. Nearly anybody will side with you when you are in the right."

Mark Twain

"God made the beauties of nature like a child playing in the sand."

Ascribed to Apollonius of Tyana

"The ineffable joy of forgiving and being forgiven forms an ecstasy that might well arouse the envy of the gods."

Elbert Hubbard

"Those undeserved joys which come uncalled and make us more pleased than grateful are they that sing."

Thoreau

"The ornament of a house is the friends who frequent it."
Ralph Waldo Emerson

"No barriers, no masses of matter however enormous, can withstand the powers of the mind; the remotest corners yield to them; all things succumb, the very Heaven itself is laid open."
Marcus Manilius

"Grief can take care of itself, but to get the full value of joy you must have somebody to divide it with."
Mark Twain

"It's not that age brings childhood back again,
Age merely shows what children we remain."

Goethe: Faust Part 1

"Age is opportunity no less
Than youth itself, though in another dress,
And as the evening twilight fades away
The sky is filled with stars, invisible by day."

Longfellow

"The great man is he who does not lose his child's-heart."

Mencius

"All who joy would win / Must share it, —
Happiness was born a Twin."

Byron: Don Juan

"If wisdom were offered me with the proviso that I should
keep it shut up and refrain from declaring it, I should refuse.
There's no delight in owning anything unshared."

Seneca

"A friend is a person with whom I may be sincere.
Before him I may think aloud."

Ralph Waldo Emerson